The Great
Saguaro Book

The Great Saguaro Book

PHOTOGRAPHY AND TEXT BY

SUSAN HAZEN-HAMMOND

Ten Speed Press
Berkeley, CA

Ten Speed Press
Post Office Box 7123
Berkeley, California 94707

Distributed in Canada by Publishers Group West, in New Zealand by
Tandem Press, in South Africa by Real Books, in Singapore and
Malaysia by Berkeley Books, and in the United Kingdom and Europe
by Airlift Books.

Design by Catherine Jacobes.

Storyteller doll on page viii by Jemez Pueblo artist Theresa Sando.

Library of Congress Cataloging-in-Publication Data:
Hazen-Hammond, Susan.
    The great saguaro book / Susan Hazen-Hammond.
        p.   cm.
    Includes bibliographical references and index.
    ISBN 0-89815-870-2
    1. Saguaro.   2. Saguaro--Pictoral works.   I. Title.
QK495.C11H39   1997
583'.56--dc21   97-6939
                                                      CIP

First printing, 1997
Printed in Hong Kong
1 2 3 4 5 6 7 8 9 10—01 00 99 98 97

To William and Beth,
with much love and
many hopes for
a long and happy life.

INTRODUCTION

Among the Saguaros, Charismatic Megaplants

ONE SUNNY DAY in February 1982, twenty-four-year-old David Grundman, a maintenance worker in Phoenix, Arizona, set out into the Sonoran Desert with a 16-gauge shotgun.

In this part of the desert, the most striking vegetation is the saguaro cactus, the largest species of cactus in the United States. In stereotyped photographs, the towering cactus flings two spiny arms into a sunset-reddened sky like an Old West desperado caught without his gun. But in fact, saguaros often grow numerous arms. Some point skyward. Others sag, circle, twist, or loop around.

That day, Grundman saw all sizes and shapes of saguaros. Some had so many bird cavities, rodent tunnels, and bullet holes in them that their trunks and arms seemed made of spiny green Swiss cheese.

Grundman picked up his gun. We will never know what he was thinking about, whether he was releasing tensions from work or using the saguaros as a substitute for someone he didn't like. But the vandal shot a small saguaro in the trunk so many times that it thudded to the ground. "The first one was easy," he called. Then he aimed the shotgun at a saguaro four times taller than he was and fired.

Before the ringing in his ears had stopped, a spiny, four-foot-long arm flew off the cactus, severed by the blast. It pinned Grundman to the ground and crushed him dead.

Grundman's death by flying cactus quickly became the lead story in the unwritten book of saguaro lore. More than a dozen years later, as I crisscrossed the Sonoran Desert, many of the scholars, desert rats, and urbanites I encountered were still talking about The Saguaro that Fought Back.

"People identify with the saguaro. It's a symbol," Ray Turner, a retired saguaro researcher, told me.  Around the world the celebrity cactus, the most photographed plant on earth, has become a symbol not just of the Sonoran Desert but of the West and the entire United States. And although thousands of other plants, including 100 Sonoran Desert species, are at greater risk for extinction, no other cactus and few other plants have produced greater or longer lasting concerns about their survival than the saguaro.

When Saguaro National Monument was established in 1933, at what is now the east unit of Saguaro National Park, it was with the goal of preserving dense stands of towering, richly armed saguaros. Yet by the early 1940s, the very saguaros that had been the reason for the monument's establishment began to ooze a black bile that ran like drops of blood down the length of their trunks and fell in pools on the ground. Then the cacti fell apart, limb by limb, victims, it was said, of a fatal disease called bacterial necrosis.

Researchers surveyed a swath of the Sonoran Desert running 200 miles north to south and 250 miles east to west and found bacterial necrosis throughout, sometimes in as many as 20 percent of mature saguaros. As announcements of the extinction of the saguaro appeared in newspapers nationwide, scientists struggled to combat the mystery ailment. They determined the causative agent, a bacterium, and the vector, a moth that tunnels into the saguaro's flesh. They reviewed the literature and found scientific accounts of the black death as early as 1889, along with newspaper reports from as early as 1904 stating that the saguaro was doomed.

In 1941 and 1942 in a large test plot, researchers cut down all affected saguaros, disinfected them, and buried them. But other saguaros in the test plot continued to develop bacterial necrosis as often as saguaros in untreated areas. In following years, scientists tried to eliminate the vector moth with pesticides. They injected antibiotics into the cacti. They amputated wounded saguaro arms. But nothing worked. Some scientists predicted the obliteration of vast stands of saguaros by the year 2000.

Then in the 1970s, two University of Arizona researchers, Warren Steenbergh and Charles Lowe, observed that outbreaks of bacterial necrosis occurred only in three groups of saguaros: the oldest, those that had endured prolonged freezes, and those that had been otherwise damaged by nature or humans. The fallen saguaros in the east unit of the monument had been old and, situated near the upper end of the species' range of elevation, had been hit especially hard by freezes.

Bacterial necrosis is not a disease, the researchers concluded. It is simply the natural bacterial decay of tissues that are already dying or dead. As Joseph R. McAuliffe, director of research at the

Desert Botanical Garden in Phoenix, told me, "Bacterial necrosis is the consequence of death due to another cause."

Still, the myth of the vanishing saguaro persists in saguaro country and beyond, and McAuliffe and other researchers continue to receive numerous calls from journalists and worried citizens. Said McAuliffe, "Ninety percent of the country still seems to believe that the saguaro is disappearing from the earth. It's not." Part of the reason for this misconception, he believes, is this: "People get excited about megaplants. Saguaros are megaplants, and they have arms, just like people. You might call them charismatic megaflora."

When I began photographing saguaros, what I noticed about them first were the technical details: they're such a flat shade of green that it takes all of a photographer's tricks to make their color come alive. And they're so tall that in order to photograph them well you need to use a ladder.

But it wasn't long before I stopped reacting to saguaros in an abstract, intellectual way and started experiencing them with my senses.

Saguaros are so tall you can grow dizzy by standing under them and looking up.

Saguaros may lack mouths, but they still make sounds. They creak and shift like trees. And when the wind blows past their spines, they make a shushing noise.

Touch the spine of a saguaro, and you will never forget its sharp prick. Run your fingers between the spines, and it will feel as if you're touching wax. Taste the sweet red pulp of the saguaro fruit, laced with thousands of tiny black seeds, and you will hunger the rest of your life for more.

Dying saguaros emit a pungent, vinegary odor so strong and distinctive that just by using your nose you could find the source blindfolded.

But all these sense responses were nothing compared to the visual delights of saguaros. In the course of a dozen trips to the Sonoran Desert, while doing the photography for this book, I traveled more than twenty thousand miles back and forth across Arizona and the Mexican state of Sonora and saw at least three million saguaros. Each had its own remarkable shape. Some resembled mythical animals. Others had arms that twisted like pinwheels or formed letters of the alphabet. Some grew in erotic poses.

At dawn, saguaros emerged from the night as exotic silhouettes. Last light and twilight offered moody possibilities for the camera.

Sometimes the urge to find just one more distinctive shape to photograph became an obsession. On the very last day in the field, after shooting fourteen thousand images, I was still finding saguaros that looked like none I had seen before.

Then there was the draw of the desert at night. One August, day after day, I chased summer storms across the desert landscape. When I found one that seemed promising, I would set out at twilight to position the camera in a way that might capture both saguaros and lightning bolts. Then I waited until lightning exploded in the hills all around me. Mesquite trees flailed in the wind. Saguaros creaked in the darkness. I stood silently among them, feeling like part of the desert myself.

The more I grew attached to saguaros, the more I appreciated the creatures whose lives are connected to them. One night, after missing a storm I'd pursued all afternoon, I discovered a woodrat's nest a few feet from a saguaro. After that, I returned several nights in a row, observing the rat as it collected fallen fruits to take home.

At Christmas time I went out night after night in Yuma, Phoenix, and Tucson to photograph saguaros covered with Christmas lights. One night, as I stood hunched over camera and tripod in the hills on the edge of Tucson, a javelina thundered past, a few yards behind me.

In the springtime, bees buzzed happily among the giant-sized white flowers. During fruiting season, saguaros turned into natural bird feeders at twilight, with birds dipping their beaks into the soft fruits on every arm. Year round, hawks perched high on saguaros so that they could peer across the countryside, searching for prey while resting from flight.

I knew that rattlesnakes lived on the desert floor among the saguaros. But in all my travels in the desert, which began long before I started this book, I had seldom seen a rattlesnake, and I grew careless. Then one hot summer day at dusk, badly overheated and struggling along in the deep gloom of an arroyo, I looked down just in time to see my foot stepping over a coiled rattlesnake. By the time the message from my eyes had registered in my brain, the snake had slipped away. After that I watched for rattlesnakes with each step.

One day, before setting up my equipment to photograph the fan-shaped top of a rare cristate saguaro, I walked over to the nearby arroyo to check for rattlesnakes. Finding none, I turned around just in time to see a pink-and-black coach-whip snake rushing away from me. When it reached a thickly spined cholla cactus, it twisted its way up the central stalk and planted itself on top of the spines deep within the protection of the cactus branches, daring me to come after it.

Another day a white-winged dove dive-bombed me. Looking up, I discovered a nest in the juncture of a saguaro's arms. Inside, two baby doves were earnestly practicing their cooing techniques.

Two summers in a row Stella Tucker, a To-hono O'odham Indian, allowed me to accompany her as she harvested saguaro fruits. One evening late in June, when the sun was about to set and the temperature had drifted down to 105 degrees, we rendezvoused at her ra-mada, an open-air shelter at a har-vesting camp that she took over from her great-aunt, whom she calls her grandmother, according to O'od-ham custom.

"When I was a little girl, we used to go by horses and wagon out to the saguaro camp. Everybody came. Now I'm the only one left in the family who comes out to stay," said Stella, a short, sturdy woman with a round face.

The saguaro fruits kept her busy. When she wasn't out harvesting, she stayed at the ramada, processing the harvest. For hours she simmered saguaro juice over a mesquite fire until it turned into a thick, reddish brown syrup that tasted like molasses. After straining the juice, she spread the

fresh pulp and seeds out to dry. And she spent hour after hour quietly pulling the minuscule seeds loose from the pulp so that she could use them to make porridge or candy or feed them to her chickens.

That evening, Stella hefted a traditional harvesting tool made of saguaro ribs onto her shoulder. Saguaro juice had stained the crosspiece red.

She and I and two young visiting relatives set out through a grove of prickly pear, jumping cholla, and saguaros. After months without replenishing the water stored in their trunks, the saguaros had pulled their pleats together like accordions.

We reached a saguaro that rose ten feet above us. It lacked arms, but the top of the cactus wore a wreath of fruits. While one of the girls held the bucket high, Stella positioned the harvesting pole and tugged.

Pods and fruits came flying down, one and two at a time. Those that missed the bucket splatted against our shoulders, heads, and arms. "It's raining," Stella laughed. "That's what my grandma used to say."

Using her thumbnail, she slit a pod open and handed me a fruit. "In the old days people used saguaro fruit to help quench thirst," she said.

Juicy and sweet, it tasted like a cross between a watermelon and a fig.

We moved from saguaro to saguaro until the bucket grew heavy, although less than half full. As we walked back towards the camp in the twilight, Stella remarked, "We O'odham people treat our saguaros as people. We consider them as people. We consider them with respect."

It was summertime, so according to O'odham custom Stella couldn't recount any traditional stories without running the risk of being bitten by a rattlesnake. But I knew from other sources the ancient legends in which a woman or a girl disappeared into the earth and reemerged as the first saguaro.

Sometimes, like that woman, I wanted to stay in the desert forever: a mysterious, solitary figure, dragging forty pounds of photography equipment and a six-foot wooden ladder from one saguaro to the next.

But the desert is a harsh lover. Moving the ladder around so I could frame my photographs just right, I was forever backing into a cholla cactus, which stings twice—once going in and again coming out. I must have pulled a thousand cholla thorns from the backs of my knees and calves.

No matter how much ice water I drank on a hot day, or how large a straw hat I wore, or how well I covered myself up to protect my skin, the sun sucked the moisture out of me, leaving me exhausted. Sometimes I grew so tired I would lie down to rest on the desert floor between shots.

One day, after standing for hours in front of a Gila woodpecker nest, I fell into the car and set off toward the nearest town. Only when I saw the look of horror in the face of an oncoming driver did I realize that I was driving in the wrong lane. The part of the highway that, in my heat-induced fuzzyheadedness, I had taken to be the shoulder was in fact the lane I was supposed to be driving in. By the time I reached a restaurant and ordered my food, I was too weak to eat and had to lay my head on the table, oblivious to the people around me who must surely have thought me drunk or mad.

Another time, after photographing all morning, driving all day, and shooting again until dark, I began the fifty-mile drive along a steep, winding road toward the nearest motel. I ignored the abyss at the edge of the road and focused determinedly on the pavement in front of me. After a while, as I stared out the windshield, which looked to my unconscious like a horizontal photograph, I caught myself thinking, "It's time to take a vertical photograph." I was just about to twist the wheel to create a vertical "shot" when I woke up. Adrenaline gushed through me and got me safely to my hotel.

After surviving enough such adventures, I decided that if saguaros were indeed people, as Stella had said, they were clearly people who were watching out for me. And I imagined that if I really did succumb to the longing to stay in the desert forever, someday someone might recount the story of the photographer who vanished into the earth and reappeared as a saguaro.

The photographs in this book are offered as an ode to these endlessly intriguing, endlessly creative megaplants.

Majestic Cactus

Four deserts stretch across the American West: the Great Basin, Mojave, Chihuahuan, and Sonoran. Saguaros grow only in the Sonoran Desert. Even there, they thrive only in highly specialized microenvironments in Arizona, in Sonora, Mexico, and in a few small pockets of southeastern California near the Colorado River. The spire-high cacti favor areas of relatively high rainfall and prefer sloping land to flat. They especially like rocky soils, with good runoff, on south-facing slopes. Here, saguaros rise out of the rocky earth in the Crater Mountains, near Ajo, Arizona.

As miners, ranchers, and other settlers moved into the Sonoran Desert in the 1800s, they disrupted the saguaro's life cycle. Chemicals from mines poisoned the soil, and woodcutters chopped down paloverde, mesquite, and other "nurse" trees, which protect young saguaros from the extremes of summer and winter weather. Cattle trampled young saguaros or ate the brush that protected them. In 1933, in one of his last

acts as president, Herbert Hoover established Saguaro
National Monument in the Rincon Mountains east of
Tucson. In 1961, portions of the Tucson Mountains
west of Tucson were added to the monument. In 1994
the monument became a national park. Here, a rare
cristate saguaro (see pages 126–128) is silhouetted
against a pink cloud at dusk in a stand of saguaros in
the west unit of Saguaro National Park.

All saguaros are classified botanically as *Carnegiea gigantea*. They can grow fifty feet high and can weigh as much as eight tons. As the largest cacti in the United States, they soar above chollas, prickly pears, brittlebush, and other desert vegetation. Here, a forest of saguaros stretches across the landscape west of Tucson, Arizona, in the west unit of Saguaro National Park.

Saguaros are believed to live as long as three centuries, but the average saguaro probably dies some-
time around its two-hundredth birthday. Struggling to
survive the sparse rainfall and intense heat of the desert,
the juvenile cacti mature slowly. In the most favorable
environments, saguaros take thirty-five years to reach
six feet. More commonly, they arrive at that height between the ages of forty-seven and sixty-seven.

About seven feet tall, this young saguaro in Tohono O'odham country is approximately sixty-five years old. At an age when human beings think about retirement, the plant has just reached maturity and is putting out its first flowers. Baboquivari, the sacred peak of the Tohono O'odham people, rises in the background.

Fewer than one seed in a thousand germinates. Two heavy, back-to-back summer rainstorms within a few days are necessary to keep the surface of the desert wet enough for germination to occur. There must also be enough light and relatively low heat. Seeds typically germinate in shady spots. Even then, the average life expectancy of a seedling is under six weeks, and fewer than one seedling in a hundred reaches its first birthday. At this point, one million seeds have produced only fifty-one established plants. They typically take between six and ten years to grow an inch tall. During that period, their biggest enemies are drought, cold, insects, and rodents. Here, a carpet of seedlings bursts from the rocky soil at the Arizona-Sonora Desert Museum.

Saguaros often develop their first arm between the ages of seventy-five and a hundred, or about the time they reach a height of fifteen feet. Initially the arm looks like a nodule or bud emerging from the side of the cactus. Often four or more years pass before the arm blossoms. The young arm at right is several years old but has not yet flowered.

This many-armed saguaro is unusual because five of its arms have forked at the top. In the northeastern fringes of the saguaro's range, in eastern Arizona, saguaros often grow more arms than in the western-most parts of the cactus' habitat, near the Colorado River. There, many saguaros remain armless through-out their lives. The tendency to grow many arms is as-sociated with areas that have colder winters and higher rainfall.

Healthy adult saguaros typically grow between two and five inches a year in the wild, but the actual growth rate varies widely from region to region and plant to plant. Most growth takes place between June and September, during the summer rainy season. In particularly favorable habitats, a typical saguaro will reach forty-six feet in height by the time it is 175 years old. In other environments it will take another sixty years or more to reach the same height. Here, two towering saguaros rub against each other in the west unit of Saguaro National Park.

For centuries the O'odham peoples of the Sonoran Desert have considered saguaros to be simply a different kind of human being. Today travelers and desert dwellers of all ethnic backgrounds continue to anthropomorphize the saguaro. With its long life span, great height, and remarkable endurance, the mighty cactus has been labeled a hero among plants. Here, two saguaros appear to embrace.

Like human beings, saguaros are the only living species in their genus. And like the evolutionary history of human beings, the evolution of the cactus is uncertain. Saguaros are believed to have evolved millions of years ago in the tropics and to have become established in their present range around eleven thousand years ago. Here, a damaged saguaro near Lake Pleasant, Arizona, resembles someone in an old-fashioned dunce cap.

For millennia, people who live among saguaros have considered them sacred, the possessors of special powers. In Sonora, some Seri Indians still bury a newborn's placenta at the base of a saguaro so that the child will have good health and a long life. The expansive saguaro shown here soars like a supernatural being above all that surrounds it.

The most widely recognized form of the saguaro, popular in art and myth, is that of a cactus with two arms rising toward the sky. Actually, only a few saguaros match this stereotyped shape.

In a poorly understood phenomenon known as twinning, some saguaros start life as a single seed that grows into two side-by-side saguaros. Others begin as two seeds and merge into a single, twin-stemmed plant. Here, although the twin on the right has lost the top of its own central trunk, it appears to be protecting its sibling. Like many other fine saguaro specimens, these grow in southern Arizona on Tohono O'odham land.

Transplanted saguaros thrive in greenhouses and protected environments as far away as Japan. But within the saguaro's natural habitat, elevation and climate restrict its range. As a subtropical species, the cactus is especially susceptible to cold. This vulnerability prevents it from spreading beyond the desert or above five thousand feet. The snakelike saguaro shown here grows at the northernmost edge of its natural distribution, near Kingman, Arizona. Note the three young arm buds emerging from the central stalk.

The segmented look of this saguaro is probably due to a genetic defect. However, segmenting can also occur following a severe frost, which is the leading precipitator of natural death in saguaros.

Severely cold weather has permanently altered the shape of this saguaro. Most adult saguaros can survive a single night of freezing weather, but if temperatures fail to warm above freezing the following day, damage or death occurs. Often growth is slowed for years to come. Young saguaros are even more vulnerable to cold. Those juveniles that survive usually grow within the shelter of a warmer microclimate created by the presence of a nearby rock face or a nurse plant such as a paloverde or ironwood tree.

A heavy freeze probably caused the unusual shape of this saguaro. In the first year following frost damage, a saguaro often produces only a few flowers and fruits. This saguaro will probably survive for decades, but even if the frost had damaged it fatally, it might have struggled to survive for as long as nine more years. The drive to reproduce is so strong that some saguaros have flowered and fruited for two years after being severed from their roots.

aguaros often take shapes reminiscent of animals, inanimate objects, or even extraterrestrials. This saguaro, suggestive of a giraffe, a unicorn, or some other mysterious beast, developed this way following heavy frost. A severe freeze causes the fluids inside a saguaro to expand and crystallize. When the temperature warms up and the cactus thaws, the damaged tissue grows mushy and sags. The upward thrust of the three new arms suggests that the damage that sculpted this saguaro occurred many years ago.

Formal scientific study of saguaros began around 1900, when the oldest saguaros alive today were already full grown. Today the saguaro is one of the most heavily studied nonfarm plants on earth. Scientists have discovered complex large-scale fluctuations in growth patterns, but they still do not understand all the factors that contribute to these variations.

People who anthropomorphize saguaros might say that this one had a sense of humor in selecting its shape.

Often each person viewing a saguaro will see something different. The saguaro shown here might be seen as a symbol of something divine. Or as a symbol of the greatness of nature and the puniness of humankind. Or as a symbol of beauty, or as a natural work of art. It might even appear sinister, when twilight makes the underside of its twisting arms glow.

Ancient legends of the desert relate that the first saguaro was created when a girl sank into the earth and reemerged as a giant cactus. The saguaro pictured here resembles an acrobatic female figure performing a headstand.

The saguaro has become a twentieth-century icon—
a metaphor for the complexity and mystery of
desert life. Here, a saguaro near the Arizona-Sonora
border spreads its arms wide.

*S*cientists hypothesize that the saguaro's need for coarse-textured, well-drained soils may help determine its southern boundary, near the Sonora-Sinaloa border. Farther north, the gravelly soil in which the saguaro shown here established itself may have helped it survive damage from machete blows.

The drooping arm of this saguaro resulted from a severe freeze. Although intolerant of cold, the saguaro can survive in colder weather than any of the other columnar cacti of North America. For this reason, it is the most northerly of all columnar cacti, which grow up and down the Americas all the way to Argentina.

The spine patterns of the saguaro help distinguish it from other cacti. So do its diverse, evocative shapes. Several feet above the ground, this saguaro has split in two.

The growth of the saguaro's central stem slows as more and more arms emerge, but the arms benefit the cactus more than added height: each arm multiplies the plant's reproductive potential.

Supporting the adult saguaro's weight are about twenty woody ribs, which grow inside the central trunk. As arms develop, ribs extend into them, too. Here, a massive saguaro soars toward the evening sky near Kingman, Arizona. In this marginal habitat, winter temperatures sink into the teens and below. The saguaro's volume and bulk allow it to retain its heat longer and avoid frost damage.

The eastern and northern limits of the saguaro mark the eastern and northern limits of the Sonoran Desert. The saguaro shown here grows in eastern Arizona, just a few miles inside the desert's eastern boundary.

Like humans, saguaros are both profoundly vulnerable and extremely tough. Destruction of the central stem of this saguaro has caused two of the existing arms to take over the stem's role. The cactus has also produced a bouquet of new arms.

Gila woodpeckers and gilded flickers have carved nest holes up and down the arms and central stem of this old saguaro. One arm droops from freeze damage, which the others have escaped. A single saguaro may hold as many as fifty woodpecker holes and still survive.

Occasionally, the central stem or arms of a saguaro will grow with a rippled effect. Such stresses as recurring freezes or droughts may produce the repetitive constrictions, or they may signal that the saguaro has difficulties growing in its particular microenvironment.

Travelers in earlier centuries considered saguaros grotesque and dubbed them "prickly horrors." This saguaro west of Tucson resembles an upside-down spider or a human hand raised toward the sky.

The saguaro pictured here seems to possess the ability to defy the laws of gravity. Eventually, it will probably fall victim to a strong wind. On windy days, visitors should stay well back from saguaros. Even a healthy-looking arm may fall. The author reports that she once photographed a saguaro and returned a few days later to photograph it in a different light, only to discover that wind had blown off several arms.

No one has ever conducted a formal census of saguaros, but scientists estimate that there are between several hundred million and a billion. Whether one in 200 million or one in a billion, this saguaro, with its arms twisted into knots, is one of a kind.

Organ Pipe Cactus National Monument, on the Arizona-Sonora border, is prime saguaro country. As in most parts of the Sonoran Desert, winter is often the best time to visit and the best time to view saguaros, because temperatures are relatively mild. However, dedicated cactus lovers and wildlife watchers will also want to visit in late spring or early summer, during flowering and fruiting season. Here, a saguaro silhouetted by a winter sunrise in the monument towers above the branches of the nurse plant it has long since outgrown.

Bountiful
Saguaro

The growing tips of the arms and central stem of a saguaro are particularly vulnerable to frost. Nature protects the tip with a woolly mat, which insulates it and reduces nocturnal heat loss. It also seals moisture in and discourages animals from gnawing on the tender new growth.

A saguaro can lose 80 percent of its body fluids and survive. During dry periods, a saguaro survives by using up its internal water supplies, causing the pleats to pull together tightly. Height also decreases slightly. Seedling saguaros often lose half of their original volume during the pre-summer drought, which occurs annually during April, May, and June. However, within eight days of the first heavy rain, the seedlings return to their former size and begin to grow again. During drought,

mature saguaros draw on their moisture reserves to produce the flowers and fruit that ensure the survival of the species.

As the saguaro replenishes its internal water stores, it swells, causing its pleats to stretch out. In a single rainstorm the roots may collect 200 gallons of water.

This saguaro has absorbed so much moisture that its pleats have nearly disappeared. Note the brown calluses that the plant produces in response to injury. They seal liquids in and prevent cold air from entering the cactus. Most of the calluses shown here probably reflect the movement of burrowing insects and their larvae.

For two months during the summer, skies cloud up most afternoons, as in the photo at right, bringing the hope of life-giving rain.

In order to gather as much water as possible during summer rains, the saguaro sends out dozens of lateral roots through the soil a foot or two beneath the surface. Its roots spread in an unseen circle twice as wide as the cactus's height, waiting like concealed nets to capture the raindrops. Growing in a particularly arid section of the desert, this saguaro has gone many months with nothing to drink.

FLOWERS

The trumpet-shaped white flowers of the saguaro typically open during the night and wither by the following afternoon. At sunrise, as shown here, the waxlike flowers reach their peak of beauty. About three inches in diameter and three inches long, the blossoms are the state flower of Arizona.

A healthy, mature saguaro can produce 200 flowers, blooming a few at a time, each spring. The flowers sprout in crownlike clusters at the top of the central trunk and on the growing ends of the arms. Within thirty to sixty days, germinated flowers metamorphose into fully ripened fruits.

As if to ensure that bees, birds, and other pollinators will be drawn to the moisture-rich saguaro flowers, nature has arranged for saguaros to bloom during the desert's driest season. Usually a saguaro opens its first blossoms in early April and continues to bloom until June, but the exact flowering time depends on location and weather conditions. Occasionally, a saguaro flowers unexpectedly in October, December, or January. Here, bees buzz among the pollen-laden flowers.

As the fruits ripen, they turn red and burst open in a scarlet display that early explorers mistook for flowers. Fruits that escape birds and human harvesters fall to the ground. Soon afterward, the summer rainy season begins, bringing with it the possibility of germination and a new cycle of life.

WILDLIFE

Because of heavy animal traffic around the base of a mature saguaro, seeds that sprout too close to the parent plant seldom survive. Coyotes aid in the saguaro's life cycle by disseminating the undigested seeds in their droppings, far from the parent plant. In one study, undigested saguaro seeds made up 95 percent of coyote droppings in July.

During the summer javelinas, also called peccaries, eat saguaro fruits daily. Like coyotes, javelinas spread the seeds in their droppings. Birds, rats, and even ants also aid in scattering the seeds. The camera captured the javelinas shown here in Saguaro National Park in midmorning, but wildlife watchers searching for javelinas will most often find them at dawn or dusk.

After dark each night this woodrat searches for food for itself and the young back home in the nest. Saguaro fruits provide moisture as well as nourishment. Woodrats also eat seedling saguaros, which consist 90 percent of water, making them natural canteens. Woodrats can subsist on a diet of tender young saguaro tissue. They also damage older saguaros by gnawing winding tunnels through the flesh. This makes the cactus more vulnerable to cold weather, drought, and high winds.

A dove takes flight from its perch among the fruits of a saguaro. From the beginning of blossoming time until the end of fruiting time—about six months of the year—the birds' lives revolve around the saguaro. They nest in the tall cactus. They sip nectar from its flowers and plunge their beaks again and again into the red fruits. And they find safety from predators unable to climb the spiny green poles.

In a nest made safe by its height and the cactus spines that surround it, two young doves practice cooing while they wait for their mother's return.

A hawk rises from a perch among the fruits of a saguaro. The cactus gives raptors a vantage point from which to hunt, even while they're resting, for rodents and other food.

A young hawk, still unable to fly, sits on a nest of sticks high in a saguaro, awaiting the return of the parent. The same stick shelter will typically be used year after year by hawks, ravens, or other large birds.

ila woodpeckers and gilded flickers peck angular tunnels into a saguaro's flesh in order to create a safe space in which to hatch and raise their young. The saguaro responds by creating a thick, barklike callus inside the hole. Here, a Gila woodpecker brings a spiny piece of food to its mate and young, which are well hidden inside the cactus about eight inches below the entryway. During the summer the temperature inside the nest is often twenty degrees cooler than the outside air.

During June, July, and August, the fruit-covered ends of saguaro arms provide a popular feeding place for curve-billed thrashers, cactus wrens, gilded flickers, purple martins, brown towhees, and other birds.

Although not directly linked to the saguaro's life cycle, numerous snakes live in saguaro country. Here, a coachwhip snake twines around the spiny branches of a teddybear cholla cactus in the middle of a saguaro grove.

NATIVE

For centuries before Europeans arrived, the Native peoples of the Sonoran Desert used the gifts of the saguaro in their daily lives. The flesh, heated over coals, soothed the pains of rheumatism. Flowers provided a gluelike sealant. After saguaros decomposed,

the calluses caused by bird nests became convenient carriers. The woody ribs of the cacti became tools, toys, splints, fire sticks, and ceremonial objects. Here, saguaros grow among the seven-hundred-year-old Salado ruins at Tonto National Monument.

Centuries ago the Hohokam Indians of southern Arizona used saguaro vinegar to etch geometric patterns in seashells. The one shown here dates to about 1100 A.D. Artisans protected the rest of the shell from the corrosive effects of the vinegar by smearing pitch on it. Then they submerged the shell in vinegar, where it

soaked for several days. Believed to be ancestors to today's O'odham peoples, the Hohokam camped among the saguaros each summer to collect and process the fruits. Excavations of ancient cactus camps suggest that cultural patterns of gathering and processing the fruits have changed little over hundreds of years.

The Tohono O'odham people of southern Arizona still harvest saguaro fruits using a traditional cactus puller made from saguaro ribs. Like their ancestors, they live temporarily in special harvesting camps. Because of the intense heat in the droughty weeks preceding the summer rains, harvesting takes place just after sunrise and just before sunset. When the first rain falls, the harvest ends. Remaining fruits are left for birds and other animals.

A traditional cactus puller is fifteen to thirty feet long and consists of two or three overlapping saguaro ribs. A short crosspiece at the end, also made of saguaro wood, tugs or pushes the fruit from the top of the arms or stem. A fundamental part of the Tohono O'odham culture, the cactus puller has given its name, *ku'ipad*, to the constellation known in English as the Big Dipper.

In the last century, saguaro syrup was a popular trade item, which the Tohono O'odham bartered for beads and other objects. Although not available commercially today, saguaro syrup is still a staple in traditional O'odham homes. For five hours during the hottest part of the day, the saguaro juice boils over an open fire until it thickens and turns to  syrup. It takes approximately twenty pounds of fruit to make one gallon of syrup. The fruit is so sweet naturally that it is unnecessary to add sugar.

The fresh, ripe saguaro fruit consists of the inedible outer receptacle and the red flesh or pulp. The taste and texture of the flesh is like a combination of watermelons and figs. Rich in vitamins, each fruit contains about thirty-four calories. In the early 1900s, Tohono O'odham harvesters collected 600,000 pounds of fruit yearly. Today, at each saguaro camp, the harvest still begins with a private thanksgiving ritual. Each harvester opens the first saguaro fruit encountered and applies the sweet red pulp to the skin over the heart. A prayer of thanksgiving follows.

For centuries saguaro fruits helped desert dwellers survive the lean months of June and July. People made jam, syrup, fruit leather, wine, and nonalcoholic beverages from the fruits. They pressed oil from the seeds or ground them into flour. Some fruits they dried for future use, like the fruits shown at lower left. While other Native peoples used calendars tied to equinoxes and solstices, the saguaro was so important to the O'odham that they based their calendar on the cactus. The first month in the Tohono O'odham calendar is *Ha:ṣañ Maṣad*, the month of saguaro harvest. The last month is *Kaij Cukulig Maṣad*, the month when saguaro fruits ripen.

In the past O'odham cooks strained the seeds from the juice with specially woven baskets. Today they strain the juice once through wire mesh, then again through flour sacking. A few seeds always slip through, adding a crunchy texture to the syrup.

A single saguaro fruit contains 2,000 to 2,500 comma-sized seeds. Before they can be ground into flour, the seeds must be separated by hand from the dried pulp in which they are embedded. In the past, the Seri Indians of the southern Sonoran Desert sometimes ate the fruits first, then defecated on flat rocks. After the desert sun had desiccated and sterilized the remains, the seeds were removed, washed, dried, and ground. This practice was known as the "second harvest."

Inside the open-air shelter that serves as a harvesting camp, a shrine protects the inhabitants and the harvest. The Catholicism that has been part of O'odham life for more than three centuries contributes such elements as rosary beads, images of saints, and holy water (in the sauerkraut jar). From ancient Tohono O'odham traditions come the altar's saguaro fruits, syrup, and a traditional "boot" or carrier salvaged from a dead saguaro. The two traditions merge in the cross, which is made of saguaro ribs and includes a dried saguaro fruit at the joining of the crosspieces.

Urban Saguaro

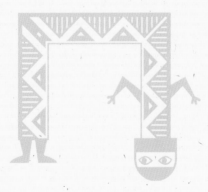

As humanity encroaches on saguaros, high-voltage electric towers dwarf the giant cacti.

Often, saguaros are replanted in areas where they once grew naturally, like these three near the shores of Lake Pleasant, a man-made lake on the outskirts of Phoenix.

For decades, homeowners in the Sonoran Desert and beyond have valued the saguaro as a decorative plant, sometimes filling their yards with transplanted cacti. One of the best-known examples of this is the Tovrea Mansion in Phoenix, where dozens of transplanted saguaros, planted unnaturally close, stand like guards in tight formation around the landmark building.

Outside a church in Ajo, Arizona, these saguaros have struggled to adapt to being transplanted. As they grow, their roots will have trouble gathering water from the area covered by concrete.

To prevent birds from drilling nest holes in a domesticated saguaro, homeowners sometimes wrap netting around it. Because this saguaro in a Scottsdale yard receives many times more water than it would in the wild, it has grown much more quickly than it would if left alone. The extra water has also made it unusually plump.

Throughout saguaro country, developers use the majestic cactus to add a Southwest touch to planned communities, golf courses, and parks. Here, a saguaro sits in a sand trap at the Boulders, in Carefree, Arizona.

As human beings continue to spread across saguaro territory, they have developed laws to protect the stately cactus. It is illegal to injure saguaros, and the cactus may not be removed from the desert, living or dead, without a permit. Before clearing homesites, builders must transplant the saguaros. Here, (top left) in a development on the outskirts of Tucson, workers prepare to remove a saguaro from a building site and replant it in a nearby yard. Cushions pad the saguaro to minimize damage to spines and epidermis.

Before a saguaro can be transplanted, its far-reaching network of roots is usually cut away. Here, (middle left) a worker uses a shovel with one hand and a motorized digger with the other.

The saguaro, now shorn of its net of roots, waits like a missile in a mobile launcher while workers dig a new hole in which to plant it. Before removing the cactus from its original location, they have taken compass readings so that the side that formerly faced north will face north again. This increases the chance of survival. Even so, many transplanted saguaros die.

The relocated saguaro stands erect in its new home. It is especially vulnerable to winds and disease during the first six months following transplanting. During that time, it must use its energy reserves to develop a new root system to anchor it into the earth. If all goes well, the new roots will replenish its water supplies, and in a season or two, blossoms will crown it again. With luck, within a few years the saguaro will produce its first arms and continue on through its normal life cycle.

Saguaro Kitsch

Throughout the Sonoran Desert and beyond, the saguaro has become a popular motif in folk arts. Here, three saguaros adorn a rug from Mexico.

The arms of this stylized saguaro seem to beckon travelers to stop and rest at a motel in Wickenburg, Arizona.

For thousands of years people have used the ribs of fallen saguaros to construct shelters or furniture. Today, stringent laws restrict removal of the ribs from the desert, but harvesting continues on both sides of the border, often illegally. Here, saguaro ribs add strength to the backs of chairs. They also ornament the mirror frame in the background.

This mock saguaro in Tucson holds up a mailbox, in careful conformity with postal regulations. In the background, natural saguaros with an uncertain future grow on undeveloped homesites.

In the Mexican state of Sonora, a friendly, humanized saguaro serves as a symbol of progress in government-sponsored billboards. On this one, a saguaro driving a Ferguson tractor is accompanied by an announcement that the state of Sonora has been free of fruit flies for the past four years.

While some homeowners in the Sonoran Desert decorate the saguaros in their yards with Christmas lights, others put up artificial cacti. At right: this holiday saguaro in Yuma was born of metal pipes and Christmas lights.

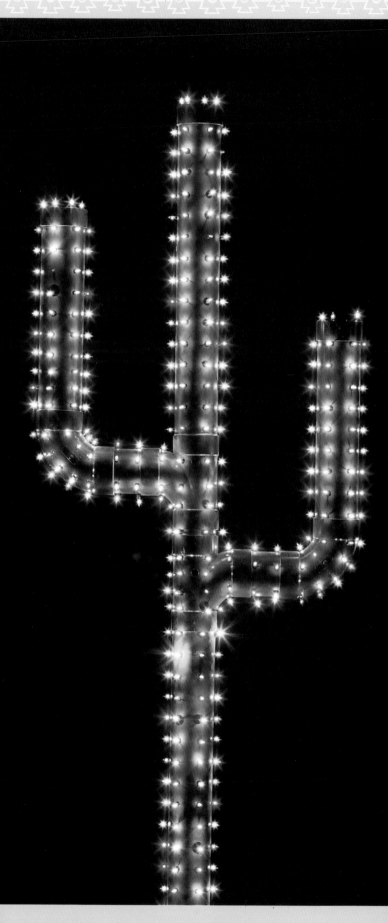

Vulnerable
Saguaro

In Arizona, officials known locally as Cactus Cops patrol the desert, hoping to thwart vandals. On page 106, a Cactus Cop studies damage caused by shotgun blasts. The fruits and the fresh arm bud are proof that the saguaro survives, but the holes in its side make it vulnerable to further damage by insects, rodents, humans, and weather.

The saguaro is unique among plants in its ability to epitomize the complex, contradictory relationship between humans and those things they feel drawn to. Each year around Arizona and Sonora, people deliberately damage thousands of saguaros. This one, in Apache country at the eastern edge of the saguaro's range, bulges around the arrow that pierces it. The wound has injured the saguaro but is unlikely to kill it.

For years, scientists and lay observers have fretted about the browning that occurs on the surface of some saguaros. Known as epidermal browning, it is often accompanied by partial or complete loss of spines. Ozone depletion, air pollution, and ultraviolet rays have all been blamed for the condition. However, most saguaro researchers now believe that epidermal browning is a normal effect of aging, exposure to extreme heat, and periods of drought.

Despite the developer's best intentions, this transplanted saguaro, once vigorous and strong, has not survived the trauma of being moved.

Before laws were enacted to protect saguaros, cactus merchants removed tens of thousands from the desert and sold them for decorative use indoors and out. Today poachers, commonly called cactus rustlers, can earn a thousand dollars or more from a single saguaro, but penalties are high. Here, rustlers have downed a saguaro illegally, then fled, leaving behind the rugs they would have used in transporting it. Severed at the roots, the cactus survived afterwards on its internal water stores, but its tightly compacted pleats show that those reserves are gone. Fatally weakened, it has begun to decompose.

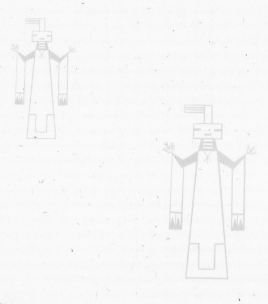

Throughout saguaro territory, humans often interact with saguaros without thinking of the best interest of the plant. Here, a would-be vaquero in northern Mexico has lassoed a saguaro's arms. The next step may be to tug the cactus down. Saguaros are sometimes killed illegally in order to harvest the ribs.

This plucky saguaro continues to grow even after most of the outer skin of its central stem has fallen away, following damage by vandals. Known as girdling, the condition will not automatically kill the saguaro, but it increases its vulnerability to wind, cold weather, and new attacks by vandals.

In spite of its shallow root system, a healthy saguaro can usually withstand the winds that accompany summer storms. But some saguaros are more vulnerable: those that have been transplanted, those that have been damaged by humans or nature, and those that grow close to roadways or parking areas. This saguaro in a shopping center in Carefree, Arizona, belonged to all three risk groups. When winds exceeded seventy-five miles per hour one August night, it toppled onto the parking lot. The shopping cart alerts drivers to the presence of the fallen giant.

Lightning strikes fewer than one saguaro in a thousand each year, but fires fueled by introduced grasses race across thousands of acres of saguaro habitat annually. Some saguaros survive the flames without long-term consequences. Others struggle along for years before succumbing. Here, a saguaro

badly damaged in a wildfire the previous summer has found the strength to produce a few flowers, but the cactus is unlikely to survive. In the background, a new fire scorches twenty thousand acres covered with saguaros near Scottsdale, Arizona.

Following damage in youth, this saguaro developed two central stems. When one died and fell off years later, the saguaro responded by producing five more arms in its place. Healthy and vigorous, they push their way up toward the sky.

In a particularly rainy year, a saguaro may draw in so much moisture that it splits open. The saguaro repairs itself by forming a callus like the one shown here.

Once treated as an infectious disease, bacterial necrosis is now considered a normal part of the decomposition process. It is the result of tissue death, rather than the cause. Here, the black liquid produced by bacterial necrosis drips slowly down the side of a damaged saguaro.

Even in death, a saguaro endures. Here, the desiccated remains of a dead saguaro resemble a science fiction mummy marching across the desert. Although variations in summer rainfall combine with other factors to create large fluctuations in the saguaro population, saguaro researchers believe that over the centuries the population remains stable. Today saguaro recruitment, as scientists call establishment of young saguaros, is up in some parts of saguaro country and down in others.

After the flesh has fallen away, the ribs of a dead saguaro may continue to stand or lie in the desert for another three decades. Here, the remnants of a dead saguaro stand silhouetted like a bronze sculpture in the sunset.

Eternal Desert

In an estimated one in 200,000 saguaros, the growing tip of a saguaro's stem or arm expands, spreads, and develops an elaborate complex of pleats and folds, creating a cristate shape. The dramatic cristate shown here stands just north of the Arizona-Sonora border.

On a cristate saguaro, the growing tip becomes a growing edge, demarcated on the convoluted crown by a thick, cream-colored line. Although other cactus species may also develop cristate shapes, no others are as eye-catching as the saguaro's. The unusually well-developed saguaro crest shown here measures more than eight feet across.

No one knows for sure why a saguaro develops the cristate form. Possible causes include genetics, frost damage, environmental factors, and mechanical damage to the growing tip. Many cristates, like the one pictured here, grow near mines.

In the Mexican portion of the Sonoran Desert, the saguaro is dwarfed by the even taller *cardón (Cereus pringlei)*. Although the cardón resembles the saguaro at a distance, it typically begins branching closer to the ground and at maturity is more massive than the saguaro. Its pleats and spinal configurations also differ from those of the saguaro. Here a forest of cardónes stretches across the desert outside Bahía Kino, along the coast of Sonora, where locals call the cardón a *sahüeso*.

The *hecho (Cereus pecten-aboriginum)* is another saguaro look-alike that grows in the southern part of the Sonoran Desert. Where the cardón appears to be an oversized saguaro, the hecho resembles a diminutive saguaro. The exterior of hecho fruits, like those shown here, consists of a spiny receptacle the size of a baseball. People living in the countryside near Alamos, Sonora, recall that in their childhood their grandmothers used the hecho receptacle to comb children's hair. Unlike ordinary combs, these combs from nature removed tangles painlessly.

During the summer rainy season, lightning creates spectacular displays for visitors to the desert. Photographers determined to capture lightning on film are urged to consider their safety first and their art second. Rain or audible thunder indicates that the lightning is too close.

The west unit of Saguaro National Park, where this scene was photographed, is an ideal place to observe summer storms.

M ature saguaros that still lack arms are sometimes referred to as "telephone pole" saguaros
because of their resemblance to that human invention.
Here, just after sunset, the full moon floats over a landscape rich in armless saguaros.

As the monarch of the desert pierces the sunset-reddened sky, the cactus becomes a symbol for the entire trans-Mississippi West, present, future, and past.

SUGGESTED READING

Alcock, John. *Sonoran Desert Summer*. Tucson: University of Arizona Press, 1990.

Hodge, Carle. *All about Saguaros*. Phoenix: Arizona Highways Related Products Section, 1991.

McAuliffe, Joseph R. *Case Study of Research, Monitoring, and Management Programs Associated with the Saguaro Cactus* (Carnegiea gigantea) *at Saguaro National Monument, Arizona*. Tucson and Denver: University of Arizona and National Park Service, Western Region, 1993.

Nabhan, Gary Paul. *Saguaro: A View of Saguaro National Monument and the Tucson Basin*. Tucson: Southwest Parks and Monuments Association, 1986.

Olin, George. *House in the Sun: A Natural History of the Sonoran Desert*, second edition. Tucson: Southwest Parks and Monuments Association, 1994.

Steenburgh, Warren F., and Charles H. Lowe. "Ecology of the Saguaro 1: The Role of Freezing Weather in a Warm-Desert Plant Population" in *Research in the Parks: Transactions of the National Park Centennial Symposium*, National Park Service Symposium Series, number one. Washington, D.C.: U.S. Dept. of the Interior, 1976.

Steenburgh, Warren F., and Charles H. Lowe. *Ecology of the Saguaro 2: Reproduction, Germination, Establishment, Growth, and Survival of the Young Plant*. National Park Service Scientific Monograph Series, Number Eight, 1977.

Stone, Charles P., and Elizabeth S. Bellantoni, editors. *Proceedings of the Symposium on Research in Saguaro National Monument*. National Park Service Rincon Institute/Southwest Parks and Monuments, May 1992.

ACKNOWLEDGMENTS

Special thanks go to the following people:

Ed Rich, whose faith in my photography became the kernel around which this book took form.

Sam Abell, for changing the way I see saguaros in particular and photography in general.

Eduardo Fuss, Judy Gordon, Walter Heilman, Charles Mann, Christine Preston, and Bill Wright for their wise input about the photography.

Stella Tucker and Edith Franklin for their generosity in allowing me to photograph the saguaro harvest and related activities.

Wendy Burroughs, Mark Dimmitt, Ruth Greenhouse, Mary Irish, Stanley Lawhead, Joseph R. McAuliffe, Jim McGinnis, Betsy Pierson, George Pingitore, Tom Rogers, and Ray Turner, for their assistance with the informational aspects of the book.

Phil Wood, Jo Ann Deck, Kirsty Melville, Mariah Bear, Catherine Jacobes, Donna Latte, and all the other fine people at Ten Speed who have brought *The Great Saguaro Book* into existence.

William Hammond, Beth Gamble, Brian Jacobs, Susan Arritt, Angela Storch, Catherine Coggan, Schia Muterperl, Elena Garcia, and, above all, Henry Mandel for their support and enthusiasm while I worked on this book.

INDEX

A

Anthropomorphic view, xv, 15–16
Arms, 10, 12, 19, 26, 35
    cristate, 5, 126–28

B

Bacterial necrosis, viii–x, 121
Big Dipper, 79
Birds, xiii, 40, 67–72, 92
Black death (bacterial necrosis), viii–x, 121
Blooming season, 61

C

Cactus Cops, 108
Cactus puller, 79
Cactus rustlers, 113
Calendar, O'odham, 81
Calluses, 54, 75, 121
Cardónes, 129
Central stem, 21, 35, 39, 41
Cholla cactus, xv
Christmas lights, 104–5
Coachwhip snakes, xiii, 72
Cold, 12, 22, 33
Columnar cacti, 33
Coyotes, 64
Creation myth, xv, 30
Cristate saguaros, 5, 126–28

D

Damage
    from birds, 40, 92
    from fire, 118–19
    from humans, vii–viii, 4, 108–9, 113–17
    from moisture, 121
Death from falling arms, vii–viii
Death of saguaros, x, 111–19, 121–23

D (continued)

Disease and bacterial necrosis, ix–x, 121
Doves, xiii, 67–68
Drought, 53

E

Epidermal browning, 110
Extinction, concern for, viii–x

F

Fire damage, 119
Flickers, gilded, 40
Flour from seeds, 82
Flowers, 58–61
Freezes, ix, 22–26, 33, 41, 52
Fruits, x, xiii–xv, 59, 62–67, 72, 78–83

G

Germination rate, 10
Gila woodpeckers, 40, 71
Gilded flickers, 40
Girdling, 116
Growing tips and frost, 42
Growth rate, 10, 13
Grundman, David, vii–viii

H

Habitat, 2, 22, 32, 33, 36, 38
Hawks, xiii, 69–70
Hazen–Hammond, Susan, 144
Hecho, 130–31
Height, 6, 7, 35
Hohokam Indians, 76–77
Hoover, Herbert, 4–5

J

Javelinas, xii, 65

K

Kitsch, 96–106
Knotted saguaro, 46–47
Ku'ipad, 79

L

Legend of origins, xv, 30
Life cycle, 6–14, 64
Lifespan, 7
Lightning, 118, 132–35
Lowe, Charles, viii

M

McAuliffe, Joseph R., ix–x

N

Native peoples, xiii–xv, 15, 74–83

O

Odor of dying saguaros, xi
O'odham people, xiii–xv, 15, 77–83
Organ Pipe Cactus National Monument, 49

P

Photographing saguaros, x–xiii, xv–xvi
Placenta burial, 18
Pleats and water supply, 53–54
Poachers, 113
Pollination, 61
Population estimate, 47

R

Rattlesnakes, xii–xiii
Reproductive drive, 25
Ribs, 36, 75, 100, 114
Roots, 53, 56

S

Saguaro National Monument, viii, 5
Saguaro National Park, 5
Saguaro that Fought Back, The, vii–viii
Scientific study, viii–x, 28
Seashells, etched, 76–77

Seasons and growth rate, 13
Seeds, 10, 82
Segmenting, 23
Seri Indians, 18, 82
Snakes, xii–xiii, 72
Sonoran Desert, viii–x, 2
Sounds made by saguaros, x
Spines, x, xv
Steenburgh, Warren, viii
Sun, hazards of, xv–xvi
Symbolic shapes, 29
Syrup, 81, 82

T

"Telephone pole" saguaros, 137
Tonto National Monument, 75
Tovrea Mansion, 90
Transplanted saguaros, 22, 89–95, 111–13
Tucker, Stella, xiii–xiv
Turner, Ray, viii
Twinning, 20

V

Vinegar, 76–77

W

Water, 52–57, 121
Weight, 6
Wildlife, xii–xiii, 40, 64–73
Wind dangers, 44, 117
Woodpecker holes, 40, 92
Woodrats, xii, 66

ABOUT THE AUTHOR

Susan Hazen-Hammond's other books include *Timelines of Native American History: Through the Centuries with Mother Earth and Father Sky* and *Chile Pepper Fever: Mine's Hotter than Yours*. Her photographs and writing have appeared in numerous publications, including *Smithsonian* magazine and *Arizona Highways*. She lives in Santa Fe, New Mexico, but considers the Sonoran Desert her second home.

RIGHT: In a dozen trips to the Sonoran Desert the author/photographer estimates that she dragged her ladder and camera equipment across more than 100 miles of compacted sand. Here, she poses for a self-portrait in front of a double cristate in southern Arizona.

LEFT: Here, her camping equipment dries after a wet night in February in Organ Pipe Cactus National Monument along the U.S.–Mexico border.